Greetings from
CARMEL
California

Greetings from
CARMEL
California

Greetings from
CARMEL
California

Greetings from
CARMEL
California

Greetings from
CARMEL
California

Greetings from
CARMEL
California

Greetings from
CARMEL
California

Greetings from
CARMEL
California

Greetings from
CARMEL
California

Greetings from
CARMEL
California

Greetings from
CARMEL
California

Greetings from
CARMEL
California

Greetings from
CARMEL
California

Greetings from
CARMEL
California

Greetings from
CARMEL
California

Greetings from
CARMEL
California

Greetings from
CARMEL
California

Greetings from
CARMEL
California

Greetings from
CARMEL
California

Greetings from
CARMEL
California

Greetings from
CARMEL
California

Greetings from
CARMEL
California

Greetings from
CARMEL
California

Greetings from
CARMEL
California

Greetings from
CARMEL
California

Greetings from
CARMEL
California

Greetings from
CARMEL
California

Greetings from
CARMEL
California

Greetings from
CARMEL
California

Greetings from
CARMEL
California

Greetings from
CARMEL
California

Greetings from
CARMEL
California

Greetings from
CARMEL
California

Greetings from
CARMEL
California

Greetings from
CARMEL
California

Greetings from
CARMEL
California

Greetings from
CARMEL
California

Greetings from
CARMEL
California

Greetings from
CARMEL
California

Greetings from
CARMEL
California

Greetings from
CARMEL
California

Greetings from
CARMEL
California

Greetings from
CARMEL
California

Greetings from
CARMEL
California

Greetings from
CARMEL
California

Greetings from
CARMEL
California

Greetings from
CARMEL
California

Greetings from
CARMEL
California

Greetings from
CARMEL
California

Greetings from
CARMEL
California

Greetings from
CARMEL
California

Greetings from
CARMEL
California

Greetings from
CARMEL
California

Greetings from
CARMEL
California

Greetings from
CARMEL
California

Greetings from
CARMEL
California

Greetings from
CARMEL
California

Greetings from
CARMEL
California

Greetings from
CARMEL
California

Greetings from
CARMEL
California

Greetings from
CARMEL
California

Greetings from
CARMEL
California

Greetings from
CARMEL
California

Greetings from
CARMEL
California

Greetings from
CARMEL
California

Greetings from
CARMEL
California

Greetings from
CARMEL
California

Greetings from
CARMEL
California

Greetings from
CARMEL
California

Greetings from
CARMEL
California

Greetings from
CARMEL
California

Greetings from
CARMEL
California

Greetings from
CARMEL
California

Greetings from
CARMEL
California

Greetings from
CARMEL
California